IT'S THE FOURTH OF JULY!

✳✳✳✳✳✳✳✳✳✳✳✳✳✳✳✳✳✳✳✳✳✳✳✳✳✳✳✳

It's the Fourth of July!

✳✳✳✳✳✳✳✳✳✳✳✳✳✳✳✳✳✳✳✳✳✳✳✳✳✳✳

STAN HOIG

✳ ✳ ✳ ✳ ✳ ✳

Illustrated with photographs and old prints

COBBLEHILL BOOKS

Dutton   New York

ILLUSTRATION CREDITS

Frank Leslie's Illustrated Newspaper, 38; *Harper's Weekly,* 34; Stan
Hoig, 2, 5 (bottom), 57, 65; *Illustrated London News,* 45; Donna
Kerr, 5 (top); *Leslie's Newspaper,* 60; Library of Congress, 18, 41,
42, 44, 45, 51, 53; New York Public Library, 14-15, 16, 26, 52;
Potter's Magazine, 10, 20; *St. Nicholas Magazine,* 12;
Daniel Smith, 7, 64.

Library of Congress Cataloging-in-Publication Data
Hoig, Stan.
It's the Fourth of July! / Stan Hoig ; illustrated with
photographs and old prints.
p.   cm.
ISBN 0-525-65175-6
1. Fourth of July celebrations—Juvenile literature.   2. Fourth of
July—Juvenile literature.   [1. Fourth of July.]   I. Title.
E286.A136   1995
394.2'684—dc20   94-34736   CIP   AC

Published in the United States by Cobblehill Books,
an affiliate of Dutton Children's Books, a division
of Penguin Books USA Inc.
375 Hudson Street,
New York, New York 10014

Designed by Mina Greenstein
Printed in the United States of America
First Edition   10   9   8   7   6   5   4   3   2   1

✳ ✳ ✳ **ACKNOWLEDGMENTS** ✳ ✳ ✳

I wish to offer special thanks to my good friend, Professor Paul Lehman, Ph.D., of the University of Central Oklahoma; to the staff of the UCO Library; to Dan Smith, director of UCO Photo Services, and his assistant, Donna Kerr; and to my wife, Patricia Corbell Hoig, for their help in the preparation of this book.

TO MEGAN AND KEEVER

✳✳✳✳✳✳ C O N T E N T S ✳✳✳✳✳✳

✳

✳

✳

✳

* * * * * * FOREWORD * * * * * *

In writing a book about the Fourth of July, one must be cautious. It is very easy to become caught up in the color, excitement, and nationalism of the subject, as we do when we celebrate the holiday. Sometimes we are prone to enjoy the festivities but overlook the real meaning of the Fourth and the Declaration of Independence.

But there is still a greater danger. That is to assume that all persons in our country have always had reason to celebrate the Fourth of July and the Declaration of Independence. Only today are many Americans coming to recognize that the Declaration's promise for mankind has not been realized by all minorities of our population.

Who can deny that there are Americans who have not seen that promise fulfilled? In our past, the dark stain of black slavery and the relentless overrunning of Indian homelands are overwhelming evidence of that. Neither can it be claimed that we have yet achieved a society in which all citizens enjoy an equal opportunity to life, liberty, and the pursuit of happiness. Fairness demands that we listen to the voices of the black person, the Native American, the Mexican American, and other minority groups, the historical treatment of whom challenges the integrity of our celebration of the Fourth of July.

We should all remember that on the Fourth of July we are not celebrating a faultless nation or perfect society. Nor can we ignore the part we each play in it. One cannot rightly honor the Declaration of Independence without acknowledging its basic tenet of respect for the rights and hopes of others. Indeed, our greatness as a nation rests upon the willingness of each citizen to do just that. Otherwise we ourselves have no call to freedom.

C. L. Sulzberger, writing in *The New York Times* on July 4, 1976, observed that: "No honest man can deny that our initial Revolution had little of the truly revolutionary, in a social sense," and that it grossly violated its pledge to many Americans. But, he noted, the great virtue of the American Revolution is that it has continued on. America is ever-changing. Still far from ideal, it is enormously improved over its beginning.

It is inescapably true that the lives of Thomas Jefferson and others who signed the Declaration of Independence betrayed their own noble words through their indulgence in slavery. Yet, under whatever condition they were issued, those words were none the less noble, embodying as they did the singular idea that all people have an inherent right to equal opportunity in life.

This concept concerning the relationship of humans to one another set a new standard in world governance, overthrowing the long-existing bondage of authoritarianism. We can only wonder what our condition would be had those words—"that all men are created equal"—never been embodied in a solemn declaration of national and personal liberty. However falsely they may have been applied in our past conduct as a nation, or are still applied today, they remain the brightest hope for people of all races.

In truth, that simple phrase enunciated by Thomas Jefferson in the Declaration of Independence and repeated by Abraham Lincoln in the Gettysburg Address, strikes to the heart of why we celebrate the Fourth of July.

IT'S THE FOURTH OF JULY!

Citizens arrive early to secure a sidewalk view of America's oldest national tradition—the Fourth of July parade.

Celebrating the Fourth

A wide-eyed youngster stands on a street curb and waves a flag as a Fourth of July parade marches by. A smiling father and mother stand proudly behind. On this day, an American tradition is being passed on, parent to child—a tradition called love of country. Each Fourth of July it is renewed; each Fourth of July it is passed on from one generation to the next.

This parade is much the same as those the parents saw as children: the waving red-white-and-blue flags, the triumphant marching bands, the uniformed service men and women, the clowns, the bicycles with their crepe-papered wheels, the dignitaries waving happily from cars, the prancing horses, the blazing red fire trucks, the floats with their patriotic themes. It is America on parade.

In Washington, D.C., the nation's capital, every day is the Fourth of July. People from all over come there. At the Vietnam Veterans Memorial they reach out to touch a name on the gleaming black wall. They walk silently among the long rows of white crosses that surround the Tomb of the Unknowns in Arlington National Cemetery. They stand back in admiration to view the sky-soaring Washington Monument. They visit the Jefferson Memorial and read the stirring words of the Declaration of Independence. And at the Lincoln Memorial they are awed by the magnificent figure of the man who freed the slaves.

July 4th, Independence Day, is our most nationalistic holiday. It celebrates the birth of our country, our freedom, and our status as a nation. As a holiday, it provides us a break in the routine of life, an escape from work, a chance to go to the lake or beach. But the Fourth is also the occasion on which we venerate our history—not only to commemorate the signing of the Declaration of Independence, but to show appreciation for our liberty and to honor those who have fought to defend it.

It was not until 1941 that Congress officially established the Fourth of July as a legal holiday. But it has been celebrated by Americans from the time that John Hancock inscribed his powerful signature on the Declaration of Independence on July 4, 1776. To some extent, it has always been a day of national unification—the one time when political, religious, and ethnic differences are put aside and citizens unite as one body, Americans all.

Yet, there have always been and still remain those for whom the mandate of freedom has not been fully realized. Slavery continued in effect for almost a century after the Declaration of Independence. Political freedom alone has not eliminated oppression. Over the years there have been similar declarations

Above: Colonial drum and flag corps is standard fare for remembrance of the nation's birthday.

Left: Sometimes it takes a sisterly boost to get a good look at a Fourth of July parade.

of independence issued by blacks, women, and farmers, seeking to rectify social and economic injustices. America's most native people continue their struggle to overcome centuries of oppression. These and other citizen bodies still strive for equitable treatment under the Constitution.

For more than two centuries, citizens have tolled bells, lighted bonfires, fired guns, ignited fireworks, offered toasts, sung songs, danced, listened to patriotic music, written and recited odes and essays, saluted flags, marched in or observed parades, made speeches, said prayers, or simply paid silent reflection in honor of the Fourth of July.

George Washington, commanding general of the Revolutionary Army and first president of the United States, still remains the nation's most honored hero. Thomas Jefferson, author and signer of the Declaration of Independence and our third president, along with other signers, are among our most highly revered historical figures. Only Abraham Lincoln, who held the nation together under the great strain of civil conflict and who emancipated the slaves, vies with them in stature.

There have been changes in our manner of celebrating. Toasting, once popular, is no longer practiced. Personal fireworks, in earlier times the delight—and danger—of children, are now greatly restricted. Over the years, new emblems of our liberty have been erected. The Washington Monument, Arlington National Cemetery, the Lincoln Memorial, the Statue of Liberty, the Tomb of the Unknowns, the Vietnam Veterans Memorial are all beloved reflections of American liberty.

The Declaration of Independence, the U.S. Constitution, and the Gettysburg Address are our most hallowed documents.

The Liberty Bell; the image of Uncle Sam; the Stars and

Boy Scouts proudly parade Old Glory before Fourth of July spectators.

Stripes; the American eagle; the Revolutionary drummer, fife, and flag carrier trio; fireworks displays; even the number thirteen signifying the thirteen original states have long been standard fare for Fourth of July celebrations. And think what the day would lose without spine-tingling patriotic music such as "The Star-Spangled Banner," "America," "God Bless America," "Stars and Stripes Forever," and, yes, even our forefathers' favorite tune, "Yankee Doodle."

Honoring those who fought in our nation's wars is a time-honored custom on the Fourth. In the early years of our nation, gratitude and respect were shown to those who participated in the Revolutionary War, 1775–81. As time passed and as new wars took place, each new generation would venerate its latest heroes. In turn, Fourth of July festivities have recognized those who served in the War of 1812–14; the Mexican War, 1846–48; the Civil War, 1861–65; the Spanish-American War, 1898; World War I, 1917–18; World War II, 1941–45; the Korean conflict, 1950–53; Vietnam, 1964–73; and most recently Operation Desert Storm of 1991.

Independence Day has a different meaning for different people. To some it signifies U.S. world prestige or American military might, to others it is economic security and prosperity, and to still others it is the memory of a lost loved one. But for all Americans the Fourth of July offers reaffirmation of self-government based upon the democratic principle of mankind's equality.

Declaring Independence

ON April 19, 1775, at Lexington, Massachusetts, colonial minutemen fired on British troops who were marching from Boston to destroy American military stores. And as the Redcoats returned to Boston after destroying supplies at Concord, they were attacked again from behind trees and walls by snipers. It was the beginning of the American Revolution.

From these skirmishes, the conflict spread throughout the thirteen colonies. There were battles at Ticonderoga, New York, at Bunker Hill in Boston, engagements in the Carolinas, and confrontations at sea. George Washington was named commander-in-chief of the Continental Army as King George sent more and more troops to America.

The First Continental Congress had been formed in 1774 to protest British measures. More and more voices were being

Skirmish at Lexington, April 19, 1775 (Potter's Magazine)

raised against "taxation without representation." King George III of England scorned a peace petition by the colonies, declaring them to be rebels. Colonists once loyal to England now began to talk of separation.

Thomas Paine, only recently migrated from England, stirred the country with his ringing cry for independence in his *Common Sense*. "Freedom has been hunted round the globe," he wrote. "O! receive the fugitive and prepare an asylum for mankind." "Give me liberty or give me death!" cried Patrick Henry of Virginia.

In the spring of 1776, delegates from the thirteen colonies met at Philadelphia as the Second Continental Congress. A motion to declare independence from England was voiced by Richard Henry Lee of Virginia on June 7. His resolution declared that "these United Colonies are and of right ought to be free and independent states." A committee of five delegates was appointed to devise a formal declaration. Had the illness of his wife not required him to leave temporarily, it is likely that Lee would have been chairman of the committee.

The Virginia member, instead, was thirty-three-year-old Thomas Jefferson. The six-foot-two, sandy-haired Virginian had attended the College of William and Mary and was well versed in the classics. He had been impressed especially by English thinkers and the ideas of John Locke on political equality and individual freedom. Earlier that spring Jefferson had written a "Declaration of Rights" for the Virginia House of Burgesses. It avowed: "That all men are born equally free and independent, and have certain inherent natural rights." The paper also contained important elements of our present Bill of Rights.

Jefferson had said little during the legislative sessions. "During the whole time I sat with him in Congress," John Adams wrote, "I never heard him utter three sentences together."

Adams, Jefferson, and Benjamin Franklin met as a subcommittee to discuss the declaration paper. At the end, it was suggested that Adams take the minutes of their meeting and prepare a formal paper. Adams declined, saying that he had "a great opinion of the elegance of the pen of Mr. Jefferson, and none at all of his own." Jefferson was appointed to take the minutes and "draw them up in form and clothe them in a proper dress."

Retiring to his quarters on the second floor of the Jacob Graff house not far from Philadelphia's State House (now Independence Hall), Jefferson began putting thoughts to paper

Desk on which the Declaration of Independence was written. After a drawing by Thomas Jefferson. (St. Nicholas Magazine)

with his quill pen. The little portable lap-desk he wrote upon, only three inches high, still exists. In a few days, he produced a draft of what would become one of the most famous documents in world history—the American Declaration of Independence.

A fateful series of events now occurred. On July 1, voting on Lee's resolution calling for independence from England began in the Congress. Nine of the colonies were in favor, with Pennsylvania and South Carolina going against the resolution. Delaware had voted no because of disagreement among its members, and delegates from New York insisted they did not have authority to vote for declaring independence. But Massachusetts' John Adams and his followers sent for an absentee Delaware delegate who favored separation from England. Caesar Rodney, ill with cancer, rode all night from his farm eighty miles away to cast his vote.

Delaware, Pennsylvania, and South Carolina now joined with the majority. With New York temporarily abstaining, Lee's resolution was passed on July 2 by a 12–0 vote. They had done it; the colonies had separated themselves from England! But there was still much to be done. The first item was to issue their Declaration of Independence.

It was suffocatingly hot in the Philadelphia State House on

July 3 and July 4 as the delegates considered Jefferson's draft. Even more annoying than the heat were ravenous flies from a nearby stable. They swarmed about the hall and bit the delegates through their silk hose below their knee breeches.

Adams and Franklin had already suggested minor changes to the declaration. Other alterations were made as Congress debated the document paragraph by paragraph. Passages that censured the English people were eliminated, but the most significant deletion concerned condemnation of the slave trade. America's greatest moral dilemma was thus left to be resolved another time.

The debate continued to the afternoon of July 4, when the discomfort of the heat and flies did much to end any bickering over details. The Declaration of Independence was unanimously accepted by the delegates. All were aware that by placing their signatures on the document, they might well be charged with treason by the British crown and face execution. After the recent uprising against England under Scotland's Bonnie Prince Charles, Scottish leaders had been beheaded in public ceremonies. The delegates knew, too, that they had set their new countrymen on a perilous course of all-out war.

John Hancock, president of the Congress, was the first to place his quill pen to the document and sign it with his large, bold signature. It is not certain just when the other fifty-five men applied their names. Charles Carroll stated that it wasn't until August 2 that he and others inked a parchment copy. Still, the document had become official on the day of balloting—July 4, 1776. Eighty copies of the original were printed that same night for selected distribution.

Following pages: Facsimile of original draft of the Declaration of Independence.

DECLARATION O

In Congres

A Declaration by the Representatives of the UNITED STATES OF AMERICA, in General Congress assembled.

When in the course of human events it becomes necessary for one people to dissolve the political bands which have connected them with another, and to assume among the powers of the earth the separate and equal station to which the laws of nature & of nature's god entitle them, a decent respect to the opinions of mankind requires that they should declare the causes which impel them to the separation.

We hold these truths to be self-evident: that all men are created equal & independent; that from that equal creation they derive rights inherent & inalienable, among which are the preservation of life, & liberty, & the pursuit of happiness; that to secure these ends, governments are instituted among men, deriving their just powers from the consent of the governed; that whenever any form of government shall become destructive of these ends, it is the right of the people to alter or to abolish it, & to institute new government, laying it's foundation on such principles & organising it's powers in such form, as to them shall seem most likely to effect their safety & happiness. prudence indeed will dictate that governments long established should not be changed for light & transient causes: and accordingly all experience hath shewn that mankind are more disposed to suffer while evils are sufferable, than to right themselves by abolishing the forms to which they are accustomed. but when a long train of abuses & usurpations [begun at a distinguished period] & pursuing invariably the same object, evinces a design to reduce them under absolute despotism, it is their right, it is their duty, to throw off such government & to provide new guards for their future security. such has been the patient sufferance of these colonies & such is now the necessity which constrains them to [expunge] their former systems of government. the history of the present king of Great Britain is a history of [unremitting] injuries and usurpations, [among which appears no solitary fact] to contradict the uniform tenor of the rest, [all of which] have in direct object the establishment of an absolute tyranny over these states. to prove this, let facts be submitted to a candid world [for the truth of which we pledge a faith yet unsullied by falsehood.]

he has refused his assent to laws the most wholesome and necessary for the public good:

he has forbidden his governors to pass laws of immediate & pressing importance, unless suspended in their operation till his assent should be obtained, and when so suspended, he has neglected utterly to attend to them.

he has refused to pass other laws for the accommodation of large districts of people unless those people would relinquish the right of representation, a right inestimable to them & formidable to tyrants only.

he has called together legislative bodies at places unusual, uncomfortable & distant from the depository of their public records, for the sole purpose of fatiguing them into compliance with his measures.

he has dissolved Representative houses repeatedly & continually for opposing with manly firmness his invasions on the rights of the people.

he has refused for a long time to cause others to be elected.

whereby the legislative powers, in the people at large for their exercise exposed to all the dangers of he has endeavored to prevent the obstructing the laws for naturali to encourage their migrations -propriations of lands:

he has suffered the administrat refusing his assent he has made judges dependan the amount of their salaries he has erected a multitude of - their swarms of officers to hara

he has kept among us in times of he has affected to render the milita he has combined with others to su tions and unacknowledged by our of legislation. for quartering for protecting them they should commit on for cutting off our trade with for imposing taxes on us withou for depriving us in many cases for transporting us beyond seas for abolishing the free system of English law and enlarging it's boundaries so as to render into these states at once

for abolishing our most import for taking away our charters, for suspending our own legislatu legislate for us in all c he has abdicated government he of his allegiance & protection he he has plundered our seas rav lives of our people: he is at this time transporting the works of death, desolation I cruelty, & perfidy unworthy he has endeavored to bring on th savages, whose known rule of all ages, sexes, & conditions he has incited treasonable in allurements of forfeiture &

he has waged cruel war again -ed rights of life & liberty in fended lives captivating & sphere, or to incur miserable practical warfare the oppo Christian king of Great B where MEN should be bo

John Hancock Fran. Lewis Rich. Stockton Fran
Robt Morris John Penn Wm Whipple Ca
Benjamin Rush Wm Paca Samuel Chase John Hart
Benj. Franklin Tho. Stone Abra Clark
Geo Taylor Geo Ross
Jno Witherspoon Button Gwinnett
Joseph Hewes Wm Floyd Lyman Hall Tho
Wm Hooper Phil. Livingston
John Morton James Wilson Fras Hopkinson Geo Walt

annihilation, have returned to
ate remaining in the mean time
without, & convulsions within:
of these states; for that purpose
eigners; refusing to pass others
ising the conditions of new ap-

[totally to cease in some of these
establishing judiciary powers:
alone, for the tenure of their offices

a self-assumed power] & sent hi
& eat out their substance;

ing armies [& ships of war]

nt of & superior to the civil power:
urisdiction foreign to our constitu
his assent to their pretended acts
armed troops among us,
punishment for any mur
nts of these states;
world;

d;

pretended offences:

mentally the forms of our governments,
themselves invested with power to
ver,
nt of his protection & waging war against us.
ng his governors & declaring us out
ts, burnt our towns & distroyed the
and other
of foreign mercenaries to compleat
eady begun with circumstances
totally
civilized nation.

our frontiers the merciless Indian
in distinguished destruction of

our fellow-citizens with the
our property

ture itself, violating it's most sa
a distant people who never of
into slavery in another hemis
eir transportation thither. this
powers, is the warfare of the
ned to keep open a market
e has prohibited his negative

for suppressing every legislative attempt to prohibit or to restrain this
execrable commerce: and that this assemblage of horrors might want no fact
of distinguished die, he is now exciting those very people to rise in arms
among us, and to purchase that liberty of which he has deprived them
by murdering the people upon whom he also obtruded them, thus paying
off former crimes committed against the liberties of one people, with crimes
which he urges them to commit against the lives of another
in every stage of these oppressions we have petitioned for redress in the most humble
terms: our repeated petitions have been answered by repeated injuries, a prince
whose character is thus marked by every act which may define a tyrant, is unfit
to be the ruler of a people who mean to be free. future ages will scarce believe
that the hardiness of one man adventured within the short compass of twelve years
only to lay a foundation so broad & undisguised for tyranny over a people fostered & fixed in principles
of freedom.

Nor have we been wanting in attentions to our British brethren. we have
warned them from time to time of attempts by their legislature to extend a juris-
-diction over these our states. we have reminded them of the circumstances
of our emigration & settlement here, no one of which could warrant so strange a
pretension: that these were effected at the expence of our own blood & treasure
unassisted by the wealth or the strength of Great Britain: that in constituting
indeed our several forms of government, we had adopted one common king, thereby
laying a foundation for perpetual league & amity with them: but that submission to their
parliament was no part of our constitution, nor ever in idea, if history may be
credited: and we appealed to their native justice & magnanimity as well as to the ties
of our common kindred to disavow these usurpations which were likely to interrupt
our connection & correspondence. they too have been deaf to the voice of justice &
of consanguinity. & when occasions have been given them by the regular course of
their laws, of removing from their councils the disturbers of our harmony, they
have by their free election re-established them in power. at this very time too they
are permitting their chief magistrate to send over not only soldiers of our common
blood, but Scotch & foreign mercenaries to invade & destroy us. these facts
have given the last stab to agonizing affection, and manly spirit bids us to re-
-nounce for ever these unfeeling brethren. we must endeavor to forget our former
love for them, and to hold them as we hold the rest of mankind, enemies in war,
in peace friends. we might have been a free & a great people together: but a commu-
nication of grandeur & of freedom it seems is below their dignity. be it so, since they
will have it: the road to happiness & to glory is open to us too; we will tread it
apart from them, and acquiesce in the necessity which denounces our
eternal separation!

We therefore the representatives of the United States of America in General Congress assembled, do in the name & by authority of the good people of these states
reject and renounce all allegiance & subjection to the kings of Great Britain
& all others who may hereafter claim by, through, or under them; we utterly
dissolve all political connection which may heretofore have sub-
-sisted between us & the people or parliament of Great Britain; and finally
we do assert and declare these colonies to be free and independant states,
and that as free & independant states they shall hereafter have power to levy
war, conclude peace, contract alliances, establish commerce & to do all other
acts and things which independant states may of right do. And for the
support of this declaration we mutually pledge to each other our lives, our
fortunes, & our sacred honour.

t Lee   Arthur Middleton   Step Hopkins   Th Jefferson
ton
ury   George Wythe   Benj Harrison   Tho Nelson jr.
     Richard Henry Lee
     Josiah Bartlett   Matthew Thornton   John Adams
Hodge   Sam Huntington   William Ellery   Roger Sherman
                                        Charles Carroll of Carrollton
Geo Clymer
     Jun
                        Wm   William   Robt Treat Paine
rs Morris   Ja   Smith   Elbridge Gerry
          Sam Adams   Oliver Wolcott

Signing of the Declaration of Independence based on 1824 oil painting by John Trumbull for rotunda of the United States Capitol.

On the day before, July 3, John Adams penned a letter to his wife, Abigail, to rejoice over the decision to secede from England. "The 2d of July," he wrote, "will be a memorable epoch in the history of America. I am apt to believe that it will be celebrated by succeeding generations as the great Anniversary Festival."

He was mistaken about the date, of course. The great day of American celebration would be July 4, the anniversary of the Declaration of Independence's approval. But Adams' suggestions as to how the day should be celebrated were prophetic.

"It ought to be commemorated," he wrote, "as the day of deliverance, by solemn acts of devotion to God Almighty. It ought to be solemnized with pomp, shows, games, sports, guns, bells, bonfires, illuminations, from one end of this continent to the other, from this time forward, forever."

On the 8th of July, 1776, the State House bell (now the Liberty Bell) summoned citizens for a public reading of the Declaration. The historic document was read aloud in the State House yard by Colonel John Nixon, commander of the Philadelphia militia. The *Maryland Gazette* reported the reaction:

> . . . a number of people, true friends to the rights and liberties of this country, attended and signified their approbation to it by loud acclamations . . . After which the coat of arms of his majesty George III, was torn to pieces and burnt . . .

On the same day in Trenton, New Jersey, the Declaration was read to a large and enthusiastic crowd.

"The people are now convinced," the *Gazette* noted, "of what we ought long since to have known, that our enemies have left us no middle way between perfect freedom and abject slavery."

Word reached New York City on July 9. Immediately all debtors imprisoned in the British Provost jail were released. George Washington, whose 28,500-man army was in camp at Bowling Green, ordered the Declaration read to each brigade. The soldiers reacted to the news by yanking the equestrian statue of King George III from its pedestal. It was said that they melted the 1,000-pound lead figure to make bullets that were used six weeks later in the Battle of Long Island.

Copies of the Declaration were slower to reach other cities. It was early August when one reached Charleston, South Carolina, and was proclaimed "amidst the acclamations of a vast concourse of people." From Maine to Georgia, it was the same. A national celebration had begun in the hearts of Americans.

John Nixon gives first public reading of the Declaration of Independence from the steps of Independence Hall on July 8, 1776. (Harper's Weekly)

THREE

Early Celebrations

THE hard task of the war was upon the new country when the first anniversary of the Declaration of Independence arrived on July 4, 1777. Battle successes had been few, and victory over England was still perilously in doubt. But the spirit of American patriots had not faltered. In Philadelphia they gathered to celebrate. U.S. ships of war and galleys, all colorfully decked in red, white, and blue, filled the harbor. At one o'clock each vessel boomed out thirteen cannon salvos in honor of the thirteen states.

An elegant dinner was served to members of Congress and other civil and military dignitaries. A Hessian band, captured from the British earlier in the battle of Trenton, performed airs. Toasts were made to liberty and to American patriots who had

Independence Hall, Philadelphia   (Potter's Magazine)

already fallen in its cause. In the streets, citizens fired small arms and shouted huzzahs. That evening, troops were reviewed by Congress and officers of the army. This was followed by the ringing of bells and a grand exhibition of fireworks.

"Thus may the Fourth of July, that glorious and ever memorable day," wrote the *Pennsylvania Gazette*, "be celebrated throughout America by the Sons of Freedom from age to age til time shall be no more. Amen and Amen."

The paper was right. July 4 immediately became a day of national celebration. Originally Boston had observed the anniversary of the March 5, 1770, Boston Massacre when British soldiers had fired into a crowd of protestors and killed five colonists. But in 1783 the city turned to celebrating the Fourth of July.

In 1788, Philadelphia, then serving as the U.S. capital, held another impressive Fourth of July celebration. The event was special because it not only commemorated the Declaration of Independence, but also the U.S. Constitution, which had recently been ratified by ten states. It was unique, also, in that it featured a parade with horse-drawn floats. One, a replica of a huge eagle, carried justices of the U.S. Supreme Court.

Philadelphia thus set the pattern for celebration of our national holiday. Other cities around the infant nation followed in kind. In 1789, New York City served as the national capital. George Washington, the great hero of the Revolution and only recently chosen as the first president of the United States, had taken up residence there. Illness prevented him from attending public exercises at St. Paul's Church. His family, however, joined by Vice President John Adams and family, were there to hear a reading of the Declaration, the presentation of thirteen toasts, and an oration by Alexander Hamilton.

In 1800, newly created Washington, D.C., was established as the nation's permanent capital. As such, it became the guardian of American democracy. Philadelphia had been the birthplace of freedom, but Washington, D.C., was the heartbeat—

the place where George Washington, John Adams, Thomas Jefferson, and other figures of the American Revolution first enacted the ideals of the Declaration of Independence and the Constitution.

Not surprisingly, government leaders in Washington were especially conscious of the Fourth of July as the key anniversary of the country. This was particularly true during those early years when there was still much skepticism in the world that the new democracy would last for long—as Abraham Lincoln noted later in his famous Gettysburg Address.

When the Fourth was celebrated at the nation's capital in 1801, President Thomas Jefferson opened the executive mansion to guests. The *Daily National Intelligencer* of Washington, D.C., reported that those who came were inspired by being in the company of the man "whose pen had traced, whose councils had recommended, and whose firmness and talents had cooperated to establish, the Declaration of Independence."

The day of celebration began in the capital with a dawn cannon salute by U.S. Navy frigates on the Potomac. During the morning the Marine Band played patriotic and festive selections on the lawn of the executive mansion, and militia units presented military drills with fixed bayonets. Refreshments were served until about two o'clock, at which time guests departed for various places of entertainment in Washington, Alexandria, and Georgetown to continue their celebrations.

This pattern of recognizing the Fourth continued in the capital under the administrations of James Madison (1809–1817) and James Monroe (1817–1825). There were exceptions, however. The burning of the White House by the British in 1814 ended the presidential receptions there for three years. And in 1817 President Monroe was in Boston, taking part in a parade and dinner feting the nation's forty-first anniversary.

Americans in small towns and even those on the far western frontier also took time to observe the day. On July 4, 1805, the Lewis and Clark expedition was making its way westward along the upper Missouri River of Montana. Lt. William Clark noted in his journal that day:

> We contrived, however, to spread not a very sumptuous but a comfortable table in honor of the day, and in the evening gave the men a drink of spirits, which was the last of our stock. And as is usual among them on all festivals, the fiddle was produced and a dance begun, which lasted 'til nine o'clock, when it was interrupted by a heavy shower of rain. They continued their merriment, however, 'til a late hour.

Americans at sea celebrated as well. James Flint, who was aboard an American vessel sailing from his native England to the United States on July 4, 1818, described such an event in his *Letters from America*.

> The 4th of July is celebrated by Americans as the anniversary of their independence, declared in 1776. The captain and seamen were disposed to be joyful in commemoration of this great event. The striped flag was displayed, guns and pistols were fired, accompanied with loud cheers. The passengers, no less enthusiastic, joined in the strongest expressions of their devotedness to the democratic form of government.

Trader Josiah Gregg was leading a Santa Fe-bound trading caravan across the plains of the Texas panhandle (then a part of Mexico) in 1831. They were camped on McNees's Creek when dawn broke on July 4. The camp soon erupted in celebration. Gregg described the scene in *Commerce of the Prairies:*

"The roar of our artillery and rifle platoons resounded from every hill, while the rumbling of the drum and the shrill whistle of the fife imparted a degree of martial interest. There was no limit to the huzzas."

By 1826 the struggling new nation had reached a significant milestone. It had survived a half-century of turbulence and insecurity. Looking to a gala celebration, the mayor of Washington, R. C. Weightman, wrote to the ex-presidents and signers of the Declaration of Independence who were still alive, inviting them to attend.

These included John Adams of Quincy, Massachusetts; Thomas Jefferson of Monticello, Virginia; James Madison of Montpelier, Virginia; James Monroe of Oak Hill, Virginia; and Charles Carroll of Carrollton, Maryland. Weightman offered to send a special delegation to escort each of them to the capital. All of the men, however, were compelled by age, health, or other reasons to send their regrets.

The reply from Thomas Jefferson, now in his eighty-third year, was poignant. In recollection of the 1776 event, the third president of the United States spoke of the "bold and doubtful election we were to make, for our country, between submission and the sword." He also defined what he conceived to be the larger meaning of the Fourth of July declaration. He contended that the government he had helped create "restores the free right to the unbounded exercise of reason, and freedom of opinion. All eyes are opened or opening to the rights of man."

On the morning of the fiftieth anniversary, July 4, 1826, volunteer companies of soldiers formed in the open area north of the president's mansion. Following an opening salvo of artillery fire, a marching salute was paid to President John Quincy Adams. The president, vice president, and heads of departments were then escorted up Pennsylvania Avenue to the Capitol and seated in the House of Representatives. The Marine Band played patriotic airs from the gallery.

A prayer was given, and then the Declaration was read by a veteran of the Revolutionary War. This was followed by an orator of the day. He noted that those supporting monarchy had claimed that the American democracy contained within itself the seeds of self-destruction and was soon to fail. But, he predicted, by the next centennial jubilee there would be universal freedom in all of America and great improvement among the European nations.

Secretary of War James Barbour spoke in tribute to Thomas Jefferson. He urged the audience to contribute to a national conscription to help the badly indebted former president who, having moved from Monticello to a second home to escape intrusive relatives and friends, was facing bankruptcy. President Adams and his cabinet led the way in going to a table that had been set up for the occasion and subscribing their contributions.

After the presidential party was escorted back to the White House, the mansion's doors were thrown open for the president and his family to receive the public at large. Another round of artillery salutes was fired at noon and again at sunset. Commemoration of the day was concluded with a fireworks display on the "plain south of the President's House."

After paying their respects to the president, a group of men reassembled across the Potomac on the home grounds of George Washington Parke Custis—now the site of Arlington

GRAND CELEBRATION!

LET THERE BE A GRAND RALLY!!

AT LONE ROCK, JULY 4, 1879.

THE PEOPLE OF LONE ROCK AND VICINITY WILL CELEBRATE THE 103d ANNIVERSARY OF AMERICAN INDEPENDENCE.

ORDER OF EXERCISES.

Firing of National Salute at Sunrise. Procession will form at 10:30 A. M., and march to the grove where the following exercises will take place. Oration by H. L. Bancroft, Reading of Declaration of Independence by Chas. Fuller; Prayer by Rev. Wm. Knapp; Singing by Glee Club and Music by Lone Rock Cornet Band and Major W. G. James' Juvenile Drum Corps, attended by Fife Major Wheeler. At one o'clock Dinner at the ⸻ two o'clock the

CALTHUMPIANS

will appear in full uniform, succeeded by horse racing, foot races, &c., &c.

Officers of the Day.

president---J. C. Bancroft; Vice Presidents---J. H. Carswell, H. L. Eaton, Buena Vista; N. L. James, Richland Center; W. Dixon, Ithaca; John Swingle, Muscoda; N. L. Snow, Avoca; S. M. Harris, Spring Green; Abe Thurber, Clyde. Marshal---J. W. Fuller; Assistant Marshal, J. O. Peebles. Chaplain--Rev. W. Knapp. Treasurer--W. G. James. Committee of arrangements--J. Wallace, L. Burroughs, F. Fuller, John X. Smith. Committee on Races---G. W. Platt, W. G. James. Committee on Singing---Henry Richardson, W. T. Pinkerton.

RACES, &C.

Three-Leg Race 150 yards $2. Go as you please, half mile, $2. Foot Race 150 yards, $2. Hurdle Race, 7 hurdles, $1. Sack Race 150 yards $2. Climbing Greased Pole 12 feet $1. Catching Greased Pig, 150 pounds, $1. Running Race, 3-year-old colts, half mile dash, $3 for first, $2 for second. Running race, half mile and repeat, $8 for first, $5 for second. Race for Farm Horses, half mile and repeat, $3 for first, $2 for second. Sweepstakes, half mile dash $8.

A good time is expected and everybody invited. The Narrow Gauge will carry passengers at half fare.

FIRE WORKS IN THE EVENING.

BY ORDER OF COMMITTEE

PROGRAM POSTER, 1879

America's independence was celebrated at Lone Rock, Wisconsin, in 1879 with a fife and drum corps, races, reading of the Declaration, and dinner.

National Cemetery. Custis, who had inherited many of the belongings of his step-grandfather, George Washington, had set up a tent for his guests.

It was the same tent under which George Washington had taken shelter fifty years before during the Revolutionary War. On occasion it had served as a banquet hall for captive English officers. After lunch, a toast was drunk to the "50th Anniversary of American Independence—a political Jubilee; may the sound of its trumpet be heard in far distant lands." An ode to the Fourth of July on the country's fiftieth year was read, and additional toasts were made to the number of thirteen.

Custis, a passionate admirer of George Washington, had decorated the walls of the tent with patriotic inscriptions. One of them read: "Adams, Jefferson, Carroll—*Patres conscripti Reipublics.*" All three of these signers of the Declaration of Independence were still alive on the morning of July 4, 1826. But the July 7 issue of the Washington *National Intelligencer* announced the startlng news: "THOMAS JEFFERSON is no more!" At ten minutes before one o'clock on July 4, the illustrious author of the Declaration of Independence had died, even as they were collecting funds for him in Washington.

Adding to the remarkable coincidence of his death exactly fifty years after the signing of the Declaration was another event of national magnitude. John Adams, the second president, had likewise breathed his last on that fiftieth anniversary day of July 4, 1826.

James Monroe, who had fought in the Revolutionary War and became our fifth president, would also die on July 4 in 1831. Fourth President James Madison died on June 28, 1836, a week prior to July 4.

As the last living signer of the Declaration of Independence,

Charles Carroll in 1826 complied with a request from the city of New York and again signed a copy of the Declaration for its archives. One of his last public acts occurred on July 4, 1828. On that date, he turned the initial shovelful of dirt in a ceremony initiating construction of the Baltimore & Ohio Railway —the first important railroad in the nation. He would live until 1832, dying at the age of ninety-five.

★★★★★★ FOUR ★★★★★★

Ups and Downs
of the Fourth

O N July 4, 1828, President John Quincy Adams headed a
unique Fourth of July parade. He and a group of American and foreign dignitaries boarded a steamboat at Washington's High Street wharf and led a long procession of barges
and other boats up the Potomac River. They were trailed along
the north bank by a large crowd that met the presidential party
on the city's west end at the site of today's Tidal Basin. Trans-
ferring to smaller boats, Adams' entourage floated up the old
Washington Canal to a spot chosen for the start of the Chesa-
peake and Ohio Canal. There the president turned the first
spade of dirt for the canal that would for many years cut through
the heart of Washington, D.C., between the Capitol Building
and the Washington Monument.

For several years after Andrew Jackson took office in 1829,

there was little official observance of the Fourth in Washington. The dawn artillery salutes from the Naval Depot continued, and the Marine Band performed on the Capitol grounds. Holiday fêtes were held separately by political groups or conducted by one of the temperance groups of the day.

It wasn't until 1847 that the administration of President James K. Polk arranged for a fireworks display on the mall south of the president's house on the evening of the Fourth. A crowd of some 15,000 people witnessed the impressive pyrotechnic display. Most impressive was a final display featuring a "Temple of Liberty" surmounted by an American eagle and the inscriptions "July 4th, 1776" and "Independence."

One of the most interesting Fourth of July celebrations ever held in the nation's capital took place in 1848. The occasion involved the laying of the cornerstone for another grandiose symbol of American independence, the Washington Monument. No one person more embodied the spirit and resolve of American liberty than did George Washington. His many admirers had long wanted to erect a fitting remembrance of him, but funds were lacking. Finally, enough money was raised to begin the project.

Families came from near and far by horse and wagon and train to take part in the dedication. Residents of Washington were looking forward to this day as the tattoo of drums and the call of bugles sounded through the city.

The streets were soon alive with excited children; clanging fire wagons drawn by stout-armed firemen in red shirts; temperance society squads carrying aloft their multicolored banners; Freemasons in full regalia; handsomely dressed military squadrons; officers on prancing mounts, many just back from battles in Mexico; uniformed bands; carriages and wagons filled with government officials; even delegations of Indian leaders from the far West. The paraders took up their positions at City Hall.

People crowded the parade route along Indiana, Pennsylvania, and Fourteenth streets. A reporter noted:

"It were long to tell of the many brightly-ribboned country bonnets which bustled and swayed about in the crowd, like poppyheads in a garden bed shaken by the wind."

Children and adults alike gaped and cheered at the sight of famous personages as they passed: President James K. Polk, Senator Sam Houston of Texas, Dolley Madison in her stylish turban headpiece, Mrs. Alexander Hamilton, former President Martin Van Buren, future President Millard Fillmore, and many other notables of the day.

The first stone of the monument, a 2,500-pound marble block, awaited on the mall south of the White House. A grandstand had been set up nearby for the honored guests. They, along with some fifteen to twenty thousand others, heard Robert C. Winthrop, Speaker of the House of Representatives, eulogize Washington and consecrate the foundation stone for the planned obelisk.

The thunder of artillery, pealing of the bells, explosion of fireworks, and parading of troops added to the day's revelry that ended with a reception in the East Room of the presidential mansion. It would be many years, however, before the monument to the man who "was first in the hearts of his countrymen" was fully realized.

Two impressive and meaningful Fourth of July ceremonies were held in the capital three years later, in 1851. One involved the presentation of a block of marble to the Washington Monument by the Sons of Temperance of the state of Pennsylvania.

The marble had been hewn from the quarries of Valley Forge, "a place ever so dear to every patriot." President Millard Fillmore led the procession of troops, Freemasons, and temperance society members to the monument site where he accepted the block.

When the oratory was done and the venerable George Washington Parke Custis was introduced to the crowd, the procession moved to City Hall. From there the president led a large company of military headed by Maj. Gen. Winfield Scott, civic groups, and Freemasons up Capitol Hill and through the north gate of the Capitol grounds. A large excavation had been prepared to receive the cornerstone for new wings that were being added to the U.S. Capitol Building.

An enormous crowd was gathered to join in the ceremony. Most had come to hear the eloquent Daniel Webster speak. And speak he did for two hours. He recalled that George Washington, himself a Mason, had stood on that very spot on September 18, 1793, fifty-eight years earlier, and laid the original cornerstone for the Capitol. Comparing the state of the union in 1851 to that of 1793, he noted the increase in states from fifteen to thirty-one. The land area of the United States had quadrupled, and the population had jumped from four million to over twenty-three million.

But there had already been talk of secession by the Southern states. Webster made a passionate appeal. "Ye men of the South," he thundered, "of all the original Southern States, what say you to all this? Are you, or any of you, ashamed of this great work of your fathers?"

But the famous orator's appeal failed to stem Southern discontent. Secession loomed on the horizon in 1860 when fifty survivors of the War of 1812 gathered on the Fourth of July at the Washington armory to reminisce. The average age of the veterans was sixty-nine. They listened to speeches, sang songs, and recited incidents of their wartime service. During the afternoon of the Fourth, a large party collected at the Custis home in Arlington for music and dancing that was frequently interrupted by the distant boom of cannon fire saluting the day.

When July 4, 1861, arrived, the war between the North and South was underway. The day began with heavy cannonading from the numerous military forts that now ringed the capital. Later in the morning, newly elected President Abraham Lincoln shared a platform on Pennsylvania Avenue in front of the White House with members of his cabinet. Gen. Winfield Scott, now commanding general of Union forces, was there also as twenty-six New York regiments marched in review and tossed him flowers as they passed.

Scott, made more famous by his victory in the war with Mexico, was the hero of the day. Eventually, however, the crowd called for the little-known new president to make a speech. The lanky backwoodsman from Illinois finally came forward—but only to say humorously that he had made a great many poor speeches and now felt relieved that his newfound "dignity" as president did not permit him to be a public speaker. The crowd laughed and applauded.

Four years and a cruel, bloody war later, Lincoln was dead. He had been assassinated by John Wilkes Booth three months before the Fourth. On July 4, 1865, national attention returned to the Gettysburg battlefield, where thousands of men had died during the three days prior to July 4, 1863, and where Lincoln had given his famous Gettysburg Address. In torrid heat on this Fourth, a cornerstone was laid at the battlefield for the Soldiers' Monument.

With the great war finally over, there was the exultation of victory throughout the North. Prolonged cheering greeted Gen. Ulysses S. Grant when he appeared on a reviewing stand at Albany, New York. There were large parades in New York City, Boston, Philadelphia, Baltimore, and other eastern cities.

But the ravaged towns of the South had little taste for celebrating the Fourth of July. Most of the celebrating there would be done by the now-freed slaves. Black freedmen held a procession and festival in Richmond, Virginia, on July 4 of 1866, while others paraded through the streets of Augusta, Georgia, in a large and enthusiastic demonstration. Nearly a century had passed since the Declaration of Independence had avowed that all men are created equal.

In the years following the war, the fervor of Fourth of July celebrations once again dissolved into a more normal routine of life. But soon there would be a great revival of American patriotism. The year 1876 would see the one-hundredth anniversary of the signing of the Declaration of Independence.

Abraham Lincoln raises the flag at Philadelphia's Independence Hall on Washington's birthday, February 22, 1861. (Harper's Weekly)

The 1876 Centennial

ORATOR L. A. Gobright was speaking at Ford's Theatre in Washington, D.C., on the occasion of the first national centennial celebration on July 4, 1876. Standing in the hall where Lincoln had been shot, he recounted some of the progress made during the first one hundred years. The nation, he noted, now reached from ocean to ocean. Its population had grown from three to forty million (one account of the day gave an increase from 2,750,000 to 44,675,000), and now there were thirty-seven states. The speaker also observed that a hundred years earlier the people had never imagined such great things as railroads, the steam engine, or the electric telegraph. Then he asked:

> My friends, in which condition will our country be one hundred years hence—the 4th of July, 1976? Will the same

form of government we now have be preserved? Will it afford the same protection of personal freedom, property and human rights? Will the proud banner still wave over a united and prosperous people? These are questions to be answered by succeeding generations.

Americans of 1876 had no more idea of the tremendous changes to be made in the ensuing century than did their forefathers of 1776. They did have, however, a strong appreciation for the liberty afforded the age to which they had been born. And, like the orator at Ford's Theatre, on this national anniversary they looked to the many blessings afforded them as free citizens.

Neither did they have, as did their descendants of 1976, the advantages of radio or television by which their celebrations could be enjoined as a national happening. Each city and community around the country conducted its own individual ceremony without much awareness of one another.

New York City began its Centennial celebration on the night of July 3, 1876, with a gigantic parade and display. City Hall featured a large allegorical painting that represented national progress of the nation's first century and likenesses of General Washington and the Goddess of Liberty. The Stars and Stripes flew from every vantage point along the streets. Merchants had decorated their storefronts, and flags hung from tenement windows or fluttered atop roofs. Red, white, and blue greeted the eye everywhere.

At night, thousands of multicolored Chinese lanterns glimmered in brilliant display in windows and on poles atop the tall buildings of New York. A high balcony overlooking Broadway was lighted with gas jets, spelling out "1776" and "1876." Po-

lice precinct stations featured strips of the national colors across their windows.

Union Square was spectacularly decorated with lanterns and streamers. In the northeast corner of the square, a pyrotechnic Centennial Tribute featured an image of George Washington beneath that of an American eagle. On one side a Continental soldier held a 1776 flag, and on the other a soldier of the day grasped a flag of 1876. Roman candles and the burst of rockets in the evening sky backdropped this extravaganza of patriotic display.

All this was preface to a grand torchlight parade. Bands, drummers, troops, and torchbearers marched down Fourth Avenue into Union Square just before midnight. They were welcomed by throngs of wildly cheering celebrants. *The New York Times* described the festivities:

> Five minutes to midnight . . . more drums, more bands . . . the plaza is a solid mass of troops . . . the guns of the fort boom out, the bells of the churches toll the hour . . . a loud clanging of street bells . . . fire-works burst out as if from a volcano . . . the cheering is wild . . . suddenly there is a hush . . . the bands cease to play . . . now a band strikes up the national air of "Hail Columbia" followed by "Yankee Doodle" . . .

But it was a choral presentation of "The Star-Spangled Banner" (not yet the national anthem) that most ignited the crowd before it began dispersing at about one o'clock. The next morning, people were back *en masse* outside the Academy of Music,

Celebration of the Centennial in Union Square in New York City (Frank Leslie's Illustrated Newspaper)

then at Fourteenth Street and Irving Place, to hear more patriotic music, a reading of the Declaration of Independence, the singing of a Centennial Ode written by William Cullen Bryant, and speeches befitting the occasion.

SEVERAL CEREMONIES were conducted in Washington, D.C., though the heat and noise of the city drove many citizens "to the woods."

In Philadelphia, a journal reported that "the day found thousands of Americans anxious to recall the events which, one hundred years ago, bequeathed to them the crown of liberty." Indeed, the Philadelphia celebration was enthusiastic. Plans had been made well ahead. On May 10, President Grant pulled a lever that sent power to a grand Centennial International Exhibition at Philadelphia's Fairmount Park. The extravaganza featured exhibits from many countries. But it was mainly a grand display of American achievement in agriculture, industry, architecture, art, education, and other endeavors. An exhibit of special public interest was Alexander Graham Bell's invention —the telephone.

People from all over the country thronged to the city where America had declared its independence a century before. Military units had been called forth to parade, and by four o'clock on the morning of the Fourth their many encampments around the city came alive. At sunrise the cannons of artillery batteries boomed out salutes to the day of commemoration. They were soon joined in their tribute by guns on men-of-war in the Delaware River, church bells, steam whistles from factories and steamboats, trumpets and martial airs, discharge of firearms, and the popping of fireworks. By seven the parade route along Broad Street had become crowded with those who had failed

In Philadelphia on July 4, 1876, troops paraded under a Centennial arch honoring the French general who fought with George Washington during the American Revolution. (Frank Leslie's Illustrated Newspaper)

to find space around the Independence Square reviewing stand on Chestnut Street opposite Independence Hall.

Ceremonies began just before the nine o'clock striking of the Liberty Bell in the Old State House. The principal dignitary of the day, commanding General of the Army William Tecumseh Sherman, mounted the huge flag-draped platform. He was accompanied by Lt. Gen. Philip Sheridan. Despite the advantage of the telegraph, neither man yet knew of the great disaster that U.S. military forces had only recently suffered in faraway Montana.

They were joined on the stand by a large number of other personages. These included acting Vice President Thomas W. Ferry of Michigan, who was standing in for President Grant; Prince Oscar of Sweden; and a bevy of governors, military officers, foreign dignitaries, government officials, churchmen, and other personages of the time. The parade featured some eight to ten thousand troops that had been brought in from various posts around the country.

Among them were units of black soldiers as well as some from Southern states. The crowd laughed and cheered when the bands struck up rebel airs from the Civil War. Following the parade, the Independence Square program was opened with the playing of a grand overture and prayers, followed by speeches. A hymn by Oliver Wendell Holmes was presented, and the noted author Bayard Taylor read "The National Ode," which he had written for the occasion.

The central feature of the affair, however, was the reading of the Declaration of Independence by Richard Henry Lee. Lee was the grandson and namesake of the noted Virginian

Paraders, searchlights, and fireworks heralded the Centennial anniversary of the Declaration of Independence at Independence Hall on the evening of July 4, 1876. (Harper's Weekly)

Richard Henry Lee reads the Declaration of Independence at Philadelphia's Centennial celebration in 1876. (Frank Leslie's Illustrated Newspaper)

who had been the seventeenth signer of the Declaration and twelfth president of the Continental Congress. The original Declaration manuscript, framed and under glass, had been sent to Philadelphia for the Centennial celebration.

No sooner had Lee finished his reading than a delegation of four women headed by Susan B. Anthony marched forth and handed Ferry a long roll. The document contained signatures to a "Declaration of Rights of the Women of the United States by the National Woman Suffrage Association, July 4, 1876." After distributing copies of their declaration through the audience, the women went to a raised platform in front of Independence Hall and read it to the crowd.

CAMBRIDGE, MARYLAND, then a village of 3,000, had even more reason to celebrate July 4, 1876. This was the two-hundredth anniversary of its founding. In Detroit, a large parade of military, business, fire department, and other civic groups braved a

Huge crowds such as this one at Philadelphia's Independence Hall celebrated America's Centennial of the Fourth of July. (Illustrated London News)

rainstorm before a crowd of 20,000, who had come to hear a reading of the Declaration. Similar exercises were conducted in Chicago, Illinois, and Utica, New York. Akron, Ohio, festivities featured the oldest man in America—Lomer Griffin, aged 117 years. He had been seventeen when the Declaration of Independence was signed.

Even in far-off Santa Fe, New Mexico Territory, the spirit of seventy-six prevailed. A dawn salute of thirteen rounds from a twelve-pound cannon at Fort Marcy and the unfurling of the Stars and Stripes began a day of fêting for the throng of Americans, Mexicans, and Pueblo Indians who crowded into the city's plaza. A procession, led by Gen. Edward Hatch and his staff in full uniform, featured a special "Car of Independence."

The large, pyramidal wagon carried thirty-nine young girls representing the thirty-eight states of the Union and the Territory of New Mexico. At the top, a beauty dressed in white with a red sash and blue tiara inscribed with the word "Liberty" represented the Goddess of Liberty. At her side was the figure of Uncle Sam, decked out in red-white-and-blue striped breeches, swallow-tailed coat, stovepipe hat, and boots. Perched on the float with them was a small boy in a brown-and-yellow suit and straw hat. He sported a flag and streamer bearing the title of "Young America."

The wagon was trailed by bands of the Ninth Cavalry of Santa Fe's St. Michael's College, and a local Mexican group. Behind these came the soldiers, then fire fighters with a miniature fire engine and hook and ladder, a large crowd of Pueblo Indians in their native dress, clownish riders wearing grotesque masks and armed with sabers atop unbridled donkeys, and floats of various merchants.

When all had arrived at the plaza, a centennial hymn was

sung and the Declaration read in both English and Spanish. Orations, poetry, toasts, and responses followed. The Pueblo Indians danced their corn dance. Then the crowd was entertained with wheelbarrow, sack, and foot races until dark, when a great fireworks display was presented.

IN CHARLESTON, SOUTH CAROLINA, Southerners still suffered the sting of their Civil War defeat sixteen years before. It was black residents alone who held a parade and a reading of the Declaration of Independence. In Selma, Alabama, only the U.S. Post Office was decorated with American flags. In Savannah, Georgia, however, the day was observed more generally than it had been since the war. Following a parade, citizens gathered on the park ground and heard the Declaration read by an army officer.

However, the Southern city of Chattanooga, Tennessee, boasted the "grandest celebration ever held south of the Ohio River" on the Fourth in 1876. A mile-and-a-half-long morning procession featured marchers from both local and visiting societies and a large number of wagons and carriages with historical and industrial representatives. The day ended with depictions of Revolutionary events and a fireworks display.

The Fourth was celebrated overseas, also. In Dublin, Geneva, Berlin, Stuttgart, and other European cities, there were parades, speeches, torchlight processions, fireworks, dinners, readings of the Declaration, singing, and toasting by Americans abroad of the great day of liberty.

THEN CAME TERRIBLE NEWS! For those in the United States who had either joined in the celebrations or read accounts of them in the newspapers of July 5, the headlines on the morning of

July 6 were a great shock. Readers learned only then that the nation whose first century they had been celebrating had recently suffered a tragic military setback.

On June 25, flamboyant Gen. George Armstrong Custer and 226 men of the Seventh Cavalry had been surrounded and massacred on the Little Bighorn River of Montana by Sioux and Cheyenne warriors. One paper described it as the "worst disaster which has ever met our troops within the memory of men now living."

Defeat of this elite U.S. military force was indeed a sobering message to an exultant nation as it began its second century.

New Emblems of Liberty

O N July 4, 1884, a highly significant event affecting the United States took place outside its borders. In an elaborate ceremony in Paris, the government of France formally presented the Statue of Liberty to the U.S. minister. However, it would be over two years before the statue stood in New York Harbor. In 1884 the creation of sculptor Frédéric Auguste Bartholdi still towered above the rooftops of Paris encased in its wooden scaffolding.

The statue was the result of a long-held dream of Bartholdi to create a grand achievement. At one time he had held plans for a lighthouse at Suez in Egypt—in the form of a beautiful woman holding high a torch. The sculpture would signify the light of Western civilization shining to the East. The lighthouse was never built, however.

It is said that his idea for a similar statue in the United States was conceived at the home of a friend. Edouard René Lefebvre de Laboulaye was a famous French legal scholar and writer who was fascinated with American democracy. In conversation, the idea came about for a monument to commemorate American freedom and a century of friendship between the United States and France.

In 1871, Bartholdi sailed to America to promote his idea and to make a personal assessment of the country. There he met American leaders of the day, including President Ulysses S. Grant. On the Fourth of July, he was escorted about Washington, D.C., by Sen. Charles Sumner. The unfinished stub of the Washington Monument was a depressing sight to the sculptor.

Bartholdi toured the country from New York to San Francisco. He found a nation that was rushing to develop itself in the eyes of the world with bustling cities, bridges, tunnels, factories, railroads, and industrious people. But there were still vast areas of raw frontier between those cities.

He also found an ideal site for his statue—Bedloe's Island in New York Harbor. It overlooked the principal entry point of immigration in the U.S. from Europe.

Returning to France, Bartholdi began his efforts to raise money for his project. Funding came very slowly. It was 1881 before appeals to merchants and French municipalities, lotteries, dinners, and other methods finally brought in the needed $400,000.

In the meantime, Bartholdi struggled to find the face and figure he desired to represent the concept of "Liberty." In the end, the face he chose was much like the prominent-jaw profile of "Liberty" on the 1879 U.S. silver dollar. For the statue's

Millions of immigrants have been welcomed to the shores of America by the Statue of Liberty. (Frank Leslie's Illustrated Newspaper)

body, he chose the model of his own mother's tall, strong figure.

The statue, *Liberty Enlightening the World*, was constructed in sections. With the engineering aid of Gustave Eiffel, creator of the Eiffel Tower, assembly of the great iron-and-copper-plate, 150-foot-high statue began in the spring of 1883. Parisians came

Left: Bartholdi's great work, the Statue of Liberty, towered above the rooftops of Paris during its construction. (Harper's Weekly)

Opposite: Workmen were dwarfed in size as they reassembled the Statue of Liberty on Bedloe's Island in New York Harbor. (Frank Leslie's Illustrated Newspaper)

to watch in awe as Bartholdi's colossal work rose higher and higher above the chimneys of the city.

After the presentation ceremony, it was disassembled into its 350 component parts and carefully crated. Seventy train cars were required to carry the 222-ton statue to the port at Rouen. There it was loaded aboard the three-masted converted warship *Isère* for its voyage to America. The ship had been painted a gleaming white, her deck boats being black with gold trim.

On June 17, 1885, the *Isère* dropped anchor off Sandy Hook. When she entered New York Harbor on the nineteenth, she was greeted by a vast armada of flag-draped boats ranging from men-of-war to small skiffs. On shore, cannons boomed in salute, and bands played patriotic songs. Steam whistles screamed, and thousands of New Yorkers lined the shoreline to wave handkerchiefs and flags.

Many of those welcoming the *Isère* were perched atop the still uncompleted base for the statue. It had taken heroic effort by Joseph Pulitzer and his *New York World* to raise money for the building of the pedestal, which in itself stood 89 feet high.

The French authorities accompanying the statue were escorted in a huge parade up New York City's Broadway to an elaborate welcoming luncheon at City Hall.

Unfortunately, the perfect weather of this occasion was not matched on October 28, 1886, when dedication ceremonies for the statue were held. President Grover Cleveland, the members of his cabinet, and their French guests—including Bartholdi and the Comte de Lesseps—were forced to stand for hours in a cold, drizzling rain in New York City's Madison Square as long military parades marched down both Fifth Avenue and Broadway.

A fleet of over 300 ships of every kind, all flying streams of colored flags, had sailed into New York Harbor to Bedloe's Island. Later in the afternoon, the president and French dignitaries arrived at the site. The Comte de Lesseps spoke on the part of France, and Sen. William M. Evarts made a lengthy address. Then, with a trembling hand, Bartholdi pulled the veil covering the face of his great statue.

When the roar of saluting cannons had subsided, President Cleveland accepted France's gift to the United States. Now

America had a great new symbol of the freedom she had proclaimed on July 4, 1776.

AT THE SAME TIME that the Statue of Liberty was being constructed, another project of American independence was seeing completion. Since 1854, the Washington Monument had stood as an ugly, blunt failure against the Washington, D.C., skyline. To many Americans it was a national shame. Finally, during the 1870s, the states of New York, New Jersey, Minnesota, and Connecticut stepped forward with appropriations. Contribution boxes during the 1876 Centennial Celebration netted another $90,000. Then the U.S. Congress voted $200,000, making it possible for work to be resumed in August, 1876.

Engineers found that the obelisk had slipped out of plumb on its old base and that the top was not exactly square. The imperfections were corrected as the shaft was continued from the 150-foot elevation to its full height of 555 feet. The line of the monument at this point can still be seen. When completed, the Washington Monument was said to be the tallest structure in the world.

A light snow had fallen and the weather was cold and clear on dedication day, February 21, 1885. A large delegation braved the biting winter wind to witness the ceremonies and hear President Chester A. Arthur dedicate the monument to "the immortal name and memory of George Washington." That night a fireworks display celebrated the event, and people gaped in awe when the north face of the marble tower was swathed with lights.

At long last, the nation had created a fitting tribute to the man whom many considered to be most responsible for the freedom it celebrated each Fourth of July.

✳✳✳✳✳ SEVEN ✳✳✳✳✳ ✳

The Fourth
in the
Twentieth Century

AMERICA, new among the nations of the world, went through great changes during the nineteenth century. Some of these changes were reflected in the way the Fourth was celebrated. The rise of temperance groups helped kill the tradition of toasting the Fourth. Women's and church groups strongly opposed this habit that involved the drinking of alcoholic beverages. In this respect and otherwise, the temperance movement did much to abate the serious drunkenness that often accompanied celebration of the Fourth.

On July 4, 1842, a country parson in New England wrote in his journal: "This is the great national jubilee, to be kept in remembrance as long as the sun and moon shall endure. It has heretofore been celebrated by drunkenness, but the temperance movement has made quite a change."

Some say humorously that toasting may have died away on its own to some degree. Toasts were originally made to the thirteen states, a drink to each state. But as states were added to the Union, it became more and more difficult to drink to such a larger number.

But even as this custom was falling away, another was developing. In 1789, the import of firecrackers from China increased; and over the years, the Fourth of July became more and more dangerous because of them. At first, most fireworks were handled by firemasters, who designed and set off elaborate patriotic displays for the public. However, by the middle of the nineteenth century, fireworks had become available for purchase by the citizenry at large. Not only did the noise increase tremendously, but so did the accidents and deaths that resulted from careless use of explosive devices.

A youngster savors her first taste of American patriotism.

Particularly at risk, and dangerous to others, were young-sters whose immaturity led them to explode fireworks reck-lessly. Throwing firecrackers behind people or under horses often seemed like harmless fun to young boys. Holding them as long as possible was a sign of courage even to some adults. Fingers were blown off, eyes put out, and faces burned. Some injuries led to tetanus, then known as lockjaw. Often fires were started, and houses destroyed. The extent of property damage, injuries, and deaths on the Fourth of July grew to staggering numbers.

Statistics collected by *The Journal of the American Medical Association* revealed that during the July 4 celebrations from 1903 through 1907, 1,153 persons had been killed and 21,520 injured. Of the latter, 187 suffered total or partial blindness; 308 lost arms, legs, or hands; and 1,076 lost one or more fingers.

Even more startling were figures published in 1910 showing that during the Fourth celebrations of 1903–1909 inclusive, 34,003 persons were killed or wounded. The death count was 1,531. These totals were compared to seven famous battles of the Revolutionary War in which there were only 1,119 killed or wounded.

In 1909, Washington, D.C., banned fireworks inside the city. It promoted a large automotive parade with prizes and held a public display of fireworks on the ellipse south of the White House. Not a single casualty was reported by any of its seven hospitals. A newspaper noted:

"Nobody's home was burned up, nobody succeeded in kill-ing himself or his neighbor; there are no incipient cases of lockjaw under observation."

Today most American communities ban the private shoot-ing of fireworks within their city limits.

Noise was another disturbing factor. The popping of fire-crackers, blasting of personal arms, booming of artillery, tolling of bells, and screech of steam whistles were too much for many people. "Going out of town to avoid the Fourth" became a common phrase. In New York the Society for the Suppression of Unnecessary Noise was organized. In particular, it sought to prevent the use of fireworks near hospitals and other public areas.

Three new states had been added to the original thirteen by 1800. During the following century, twenty-nine more came into the Union to make forty-five. Then came Oklahoma in 1907, New Mexico in 1912, and Arizona in 1912 to fill out the continental United States from coast to coast. Admission of each new state brought renewed remembrance of the nation's founding. It was fitting that the admissions of Alaska, the forty-ninth state, on January 3, 1959, and Hawaii, the fiftieth, on August 21, 1959, were both celebrated on the following July 4.

American patriotism would fluctuate to extremes during the twentieth century. It would rise to great heights during World War I and World War II. But it would dip to new lows during the Great Depression of the 1930s and during the bitterly divisive and lengthy Vietnam conflict. Without doubt, patriotic fervor was at its zenith during the Bicentennial celebration of 1976.

This was unquestionably America's most grandiose Fourth of July celebration. United in a common experience by television, citizens throughout the nation marveled as one at the sight of the majestic tall ships that came from around the world and paraded up the Hudson River. Viewing Americans by the millions joined the enthusiastic 400,000 along Boston's Esplanade in hearing the Boston Pops' stirring Fourth of July concert.

On Independence Day in 1887, the United States reached from coast to coast. (Leslie's Newspaper)

The nation's two-hundredth birthday began with a flag-raising ceremony atop Mars Hill Mountain in Maine. In Baltimore Harbor at Fort McHenry, where Francis Scott Key wrote his famous words for "The Star-Spangled Banner," the dawn was greeted by the proud strains of the national anthem. In Philadelphia, descendants of participants in the American Revolution symbolically laid hands upon the Liberty Bell together. President Gerald Ford addressed a crowded Independence Hall.

Bells rang out in fifty states and in American communities abroad. Washington, D.C., saw its greatest fireworks ever, while in the town of George, state of Washington, citizens proudly displayed the largest cherry pie (69,000 pounds) ever made. All around the nation and the world, Americans were electronic witnesses to the stupendous fireworks displays surrounding the Statue of Liberty in New York Harbor and the Washington Monument in the nation's capital.

During the year of celebration, history was recreated at historic sites and communities throughout the country, each commemorating an event or accomplishment relating to the national experience. Under the auspices of the American Revolution Bicentennial Commission, over 30,000 projects and events were undertaken by various groups. These included citizen involvement in an almost endless variety of exhibits, historical reenactments and restoration, tours, trails, wagon trains, pageants, living histories, student art and literary contests, ethnic events, lectures, publications, rodeos, dioramas, coining of commemorative medallions, burying of time capsules, and many other events.

When originally formed in 1970, the Bicentennial Commission had urged all groups to reexamine the origins, values, and meaning of America. It also encouraged Americans to help make their nation the "more perfect union" that it originally sought to be. As the end of the twentieth century approaches, it has become more and more evident that this is an unending task. Not all Americans have seen the Fourth of July in the same light.

Minorities and the Fourth

O N July 5, 1852—nine years before the outbreak of the Civil War—Frederick Douglass was invited to speak at a public celebration of the Fourth of July in Rochester, New York. The great black orator was eloquent, and he did not mince words. He told his essentially white audience: "The blessings in which you, this day, rejoice, are not enjoyed in common . . . The Fourth of July is yours, not mine."

Douglass went on to define the horrors of slavery and the hypocrisy of a nation that supported it.

> Would you have me argue that man is entitled to liberty? That he is the rightful owner of his own body? You have already declared it . . . am I to argue that it is wrong to make men brutes, to rob them of liberty, to work them without wages, to keep them ignorant of the relations to their fellow

men, to beat them with sticks, to flay their flesh with the lash, to load their limbs with irons, to hunt them with dogs, to burn their flesh, to starve them into obedience and submission to their masters?

Lincoln's Emancipation Proclamation, issued on New Year's Day, 1863, declared freedom for the slaves then held in the rebellious Southern states, though it would later require the Thirteenth Amendment to the Constitution in 1865 to free all slaves. On July 4, 1864, grateful Baltimore black citizens collected money among themselves and presented Lincoln with a beautiful Bible costing $5,800. Still, in 1876 when abolitionist William Lloyd Garrison wrote his "Centennial Reflections," he was compelled to observe: "The melancholy fact is that the nation has never repented of its great transgression."

During the course of the two-plus centuries since issuance of the Declaration and writing of the Constitution, many Americans have sought the justice that these documents promise. As early as 1777, a group of black slaves petitioned for their right to the freedom that "the Great Parent of the Universe bestowed equally upon mankind."

Even today many black people in the West celebrate what became known in Texas as "Juneteenth"—June 19th, 1863, being the date that news of Lincoln's Emancipation Proclamation and their declared liberation reached Galveston, Texas, by ship.

In 1848, even before Susan B. Anthony's declaration of women's rights in 1876, a Woman's Rights Convention at Seneca Falls, New York, had issued a "Declaration of Sentiments of the Woman's Rights." Repeating the ideology of the Declaration, it stated: "We hold these truths to be self-evident: that all men and women are created equal . . ." The declaration listed the numerous restrictions on women under American laws of the day—the inability to vote and their condition in other areas being primary. It would be 1919 before the Nineteenth Amendment to the Constitution gave suffrage to American women.

Freedom was expressed in economic terms during a farmers' rebellion in 1873. On Independence Day that year the National Granger Movement issued what was known as "The Farmers' Declaration of Independence." High farm costs and small profits had brought farmers' demands for government regulation of railroads and grain elevators. The farmers' document argued their right to throw off the tyranny of laws that permitted monopolies to wring their wealth from them.

Left: A weary Independence Day celebrant finds comfort on her mother's shoulder.

Opposite: Pridefully patriotic, Native Americans incorporate the Stars and Stripes into their tribal ceremonies.

Most Native Americans readily join in the celebration of the Fourth of July with dances and powwows. Their relationship to the day, however, is far from that of other segments of society. It is not to be expected that a race that has suffered as much loss as they have would celebrate America's treatment of them. To many of them the founding fathers and those who followed were conquerors, not liberators. For them, a large part of celebrating the Fourth involves paying respect to their ancestors and to their love of the Mother Earth. It also provides a special opportunity to honor their young men and women, living and dead, who have served so bravely in America's wars.

William Lloyd Garrison pointed to the fact that Washington, Jefferson, and Patrick Henry were all slave holders; that signer Charles Carroll, one of the richest men in America, "left a thousand slaves to his heirs, liberating none!" Garrison then quoted the classic Shakespearean lines from *Julius Caesar*:

"The evil that men do lives after them.
The good is oft interred with their bones."

In truth, however, the opposite could well be said of the signers of the Declaration of Independence. Their deeds have long since been buried with them. But their avowal that "all men are created equal" lives on as the greatest hope of freedom for all humanity.

It is the fundamental reason that we celebrate the Fourth of July.

✳ ✳

IN CONGRESS, July 4, 1776
A DECLARATION
By the Representatives of the
UNITED STATES OF AMERICA
In General Congress assembled

When in the Course of human Events, it becomes necessary for one People to dissolve the Political Bands which have connected them with another, and to assume among the Powers of the Earth, the separate and equal Station to which the Laws of Nature and of Nature's God entitle them, a decent Respect to the Opinions of Mankind requires that they should declare the causes which impel them to the Separation.

We hold these Truths to be self-evident, that all Men are created equal, that they are endowed by their Creator with certain unalienable Rights, that among these are Life, Liberty, and the Pursuit of Happiness—That to secure these Rights, Governments are instituted among Men, deriving their just Powers from the Consent of the Governed, that whenever any Form of Government becomes destructive of these Ends, it is the Right of the People to alter or to abolish it, and to institute new Government, laying its Foundation on such Principles, and organizing its Powers in such Form, as to them shall seem most likely to effect their Safety and Happiness. Prudence, indeed, will dictate that Governments long established should not be changed for light and transient Causes; and accordingly all Experience hath shewn, that Mankind are more disposed to suffer, while Evils are sufferable, than to right themselves by abolishing the Forms to which they are accustomed. But when a long Train of Abuses and Usurpations, pursuing invariably the same Object, evinces a Design to reduce them under absolute Despotism, it is their Right, it is their Duty, to throw off such Government, and to provide new Guards for their future Security. Such has been the patient Sufferance of these Colonies; and such is now the Necessity which constrains them to alter their former systems of Government. The History of the present King of Great-Britain is a History of repeated Injuries and Usurpations, all having in direct Object the Establishment of an absolute Tyranny over these States. To prove this, let Facts be submitted to a candid World.

He has refused his Assent to Laws, the most wholesome and necessary for the public Good.

He has forbidden his Governors to pass Laws of immediate and pressing Importance, unless suspended in their Operation till his Assent should be obtained; and when so suspended, he has utterly neglected to attend to them.

He has refused to pass other Laws for the Accommodation of large Districts of People, unless those People would relinquish the Right of Representation in the Legislature, a Right inestimable to them, and formidable to Tyrants only.

He has called together Legislative Bodies at Places unusual, uncomfortable and distant from the Depository of their Public Records, for the sole Purpose of fatiguing them into Compliance with his Measures.

He has dissolved Representative Houses repeatedly, for opposing with manly Firmness his Invasions on the Rights of the People.

He has refused for a long Time, after such Dissolutions, to cause others to be elected; whereby the Legislative Powers, incapable of Annihilation, have returned to the People at large for their exercise; the State remaining in the mean time exposed to all the Dangers of Invasion from without, and Convulsions within.

He has endeavoured to prevent the Population of these States; for that Purpose obstructing the Laws of Naturalization of Foreigners;

refusing to pass others to encourage their Migrations hither, and raising the Conditions of new Appropriations of Lands.

He has obstructed the Administration of Justice, by refusing his Assent to Laws for establishing Judiciary Powers.

He has made Judges dependent on his Will alone, for the Tenure of their Offices, and the Amount and payment of their Salaries.

He has erected a Multitude of new Offices, and sent hither Swarms of Officers to harass our People, and eat out their Substance.

He has kept among us, in Times of Peace, Standing Armies, without the consent of our Legislatures.

He has affected to render the Military independent of, and superior to the Civil Power.

He has combined with others to subject us to a Jurisdiction foreign to our Constitution, and unacknowledged by our Laws; giving his Assent to their Acts of pretended Legislation:

For quartering large Bodies of Armed Troops among us:

For protecting them, by a mock Trial, from Punishment for any Murders which they should commit on the Inhabitants of these States:

For cutting off our Trade with all Parts of the World:

For imposing Taxes on us without our Consent:

For depriving us, in many Cases, of the Benefits of Trial by Jury:

For transporting us beyond Seas to be tried for pretended Offences:

For abolishing the free System of English Laws in a neighbouring Province, establishing therein an arbitrary Government, and enlarging its Boundaries, so as to render it at once an Example and fit Instrument for introducing the same absoute Rule into these Colonies:

For taking away our Charters, abolishing our most valuable Laws, and altering fundamentally the Forms of our Governments:

For suspending our own Legislatures, and declaring themselves invested with Power to legislate for us in all Cases whatsoever.

He has abdicated Government here, by declaring us out of his Protection and waging War against us.

He has plundered our Seas, ravaged our Coasts, burnt our towns, and destroyed the Lives of our People.

He is, at this Time, transporting large Armies of foreign Mercenaries to complete the works of Death, Desolation, and Tyranny, already begun with circumstances of Cruelty and Perfidy, scarcely paralleled in the most barbarous Ages, and totally unworthy the Head of a civilized Nation.

He has constrained our fellow Citizens taken Captive on the high Seas to bear Arms against their Country, to become the Executioners of their Friends and Brethern, or to fall themselves by their Hands.

He has excited domestic Insurrections amongst us, and has endeavoured to bring on the Inhabitants of our Frontiers, the merciless Indian Savages, whose known Rule of Warfare, is an undistinguished Destruction, of all Ages, Sexes and Conditions.

In every stage of these Oppressions we have Petitioned for Redress in the most humble Terms: Our repeated Petitions have been answered only by repeated Injury. A Prince, whose Character is thus marked by every act which may define a Tyrant, is unfit to be the Ruler of a free People.

Nor have we been wanting in Attentions to our British Brethern. We have warned them from Time to Time of Attempts by their Legislature to extend an unwarrantable Jurisdiction over us. We have reminded them of the Circumstances of our Emigration and Settlement here. We have appealed to their native Justice and Magnanimity, and we have conjured them by the Ties of our common Kindred to disavow these Usurpations, which, would inevitably interrupt our Connections and Correspondence. They too have been deaf to the Voice of Justice and of Consanguinity. We must, therefore, acquiesce in the Necessity, which denounces our Separation, and hold them, as we hold the rest of Mankind, Enemies in War, in Peace, Friends.

We, therefore, the Representatives of the UNITED STATES

OF AMERICA, in General Congress, Assembled, appealing to the Supreme Judge of the World for the Rectitude of our Intentions, do, in the Name, and by Authority of the good People of these Colonies, solemnly Publish and Declare, That these United Colonies are, and of Right ought to be, Free and Independent States; that they are absolved from all Allegiance to the British Crown, and that all political Connection between them and the State of Great-Britain, is and ought to be totally dissolved; and that as Free and Independent States, they have full Power to levy War, conclude Peace, contract Alliances, establish Commerce, and to do all other Acts and Things which Independent States may of right do. And for the support of this declaration, with a firm Reliance on the Protection of divine Providence, we mutually pledge to each other our lives, our Fortunes, and our sacred Honor.

JOHN HANCOCK, President

Attest.
CHARLES THOMSON, Secretary

✴ ✴ ✴ ✴ ✴ BIBLIOGRAPHY ✴ ✴ ✴ ✴ ✴

ARTICLES

Crane, Frank. "The Old-Time Fourth," *Outlook*, June 20, 1876: 1145–46.

"A Century of Firecrackers," *Harper's Weekly*, July 2, 1910: 29.

"The Day We Celebrate," *Atlantic*, July 1904: 108–13.

Deloria, Vine, Jr. "A Last Word from the First Americans," *The New York Times*, July 4, 1976.

Haworth, Paul Leland. "The Real Fourth of July," *Harper's Monthly*, July 1905: 214–16.

Howe, Julia Ward. "How the Fourth of July Should Be Celebrated," *Forum*, July 1893: 567–74.

"Liberty's Welcome," *Frank Leslie's Illustrated Newspaper*, June 27, 1885: 303.

Morris, Nellie Hess. "The Birth of the American Republic," *Potter's American Monthly*, July 1875: 491–504.

"On Keeping the Fourth of July," *Atlantic Monthly*, July 1902: 1–5.

"One Hundred Years, Centenary of American Independence," *Frank Leslie's Illustrated Newspaper*, July 22, 1876.

"Our Murderous Patriotism," *Harper's Weekly*, June 11, 1910: 24.

Quarles, Benjamin. "Antebellum Free Black and the Spirit of '76," *Journal of Negro History*, 61, 3 (1976): 229–242.

Lossing, Benson J. "The Historic Buildings of America," *Potter's American Monthly*, July 1876: 2–8.

Rice, Mrs. Isaac L. "Our Barbarous Fourth," *Century*, June 1908: 219–23.

Rosewater, Victor. "The One Hundred and Fiftieth Fourth," *Forum*, July 1922: 597–605.

"1775—Lexington and Concord—1875," *Potter's American Monthly*, April 1875: 250–56.

"The Statue of Liberty," *Harper's Weekly*, November 6, 1886: 714.

"The Story of the Signing," *Scribner's Monthly*, XII, 3 (July 1876): 289–301.

Sulzberger, C. L. "The Flawed American Revolution," *The New York Times*, July 4, 1976.

"The Supreme Event in American History," *Leslie's Weekly*, July 10, 1902: 35–36.

Sweet, Leonard I. "The 4th of July and Black America in the 19th Century," *Journal of Negro History*, 61, 3 (1976): 256–275.

White, Frank Marshal. "The 'Fourth' in New York One Hundred Years Ago," *Harper's Weekly*, July 6, 1907: 982.

BOOKS

Centennial Celebration at Sante Fe, New Mexico, Western History Collection, Yale University Library Microfilm Series, No. 4755.

Comprehensive Calendar of Bicentennial Events. Washington: American Revolution Bicentennial Administration, September 1976.

Dalgliesh, Alice. *The Fourth of July Story*. New York: Scribner, 1956.

Davis, Arthur P. and Saunder Redding, eds. *Cavalcade: Negro American Writing from 1760 to the Present*. Boston: Houghton Mifflin Co., 1971.

Flint, James. *Letters from America, 1818–1820.* Reuben Gold Thwaites, ed., *Early Western Travels*, IX; Cleveland: Arthur H. Clark Co., 1904.

Giblin, James. *Fireworks, Picnics, and Flags.* New York: Clarion Books, 1983.

Graham-Barber, Lynda. *Doodle Dandy! The Complete List of Independence Day Words.* New York: Bradbury Press, 1992.

Gregg, Josiah. *Commerce of the Prairie.* Max L. Moorhead, ed. Norman: University of Oklahoma Press, 1954.

Hamlin, Oscar, and eds. *Statue of Liberty.* New York: Newsweek Book Division, 1971.

Harris, Jonathan. *A Statue for America.* New York: Macmillan, 1985.

Lewis and Clark Journals, Western History Collection, Yale University Library Microfilm Series, No. 3236.

Mercer, Charles. *Statue of Liberty.* G. P. Putnam's Sons, 1979.

Phelan, Mary Kay. *The Fourth of July.* New York: Crowell, 1966.

Schauffler, Robert Haven, ed. *Independence Day: Its Celebration, Spirit, and Significance in Prose and Verse.* New York: Dodd, Mead and Co., 1912.

NEWSPAPERS

Daily National Intelligencer (Washington, D.C.)

The New York Times

The Independent (New York)

Harper's Weekly

Washington Evening Star

Illustrated London News

St. Louis Post Dispatch

St. Louis Democrat

Maryland Gazette (Baltimore)

The Times (London)

Washington Evening Star

*****INDEX*****